# CONTENTS

# MADE IN BRITAIN

Queen Victoria came to the throne in 1837, at the age of eighteen, and reigned over Great Britain until her death in 1901. During her life, enormous changes took place, the most dramatic of which was Britain's transformation from a farming country into a rich industrial nation. When Victoria was born there were about 14 million people in England, Scotland and Wales. Most of these lived and worked in the countryside. By the time the Queen died, this population had risen to over 37 million, most of whom lived in or near rapidly expanding cities and towns, and worked in factories, offices and shops.

▲This photograph shows the inside of a Victorian bicycle factory. Photography was invented in the 1820s and 30s, but the cheap portable kodak box camera didn't appear until 1888.

In Victorian times Great Britain included all of Ireland as well as Scotland, England and Wales.

# FULL STEAM AHEAD

Britain's growth as a great industrial and manufacturing nation was largely due to the improvement of the steam engine in the 1780s. Before steam engines were invented, machines could only be powered by wind, water, people or horses. Machines driven by steam were not only more reliable, they were quicker too. Not surprisingly, smart businessmen soon realised that by using steam-powered machinery they could produce goods more cheaply than ever before. So they built factories to house the monstrous new machines and employed lots of people to work in them.

◄ 'Iron and Coal' by W. Bell Scott. The Victorians used steam to power trains and ships as well as furnaces and factory machinery. How many uses for steam can you see in this picture?

Some Victorian farmers bought steam-powered machines to help them produce the extra food needed to feed Britain's growing population. These machines meant that fewer workers were needed, so many farm hands moved to the cities and towns that were springing up around factories to find work.

# ON THE RAILS

When Victoria was a child, few people travelled far from home. Those that did usually set off on foot or horseback, or rode along rutted roads in a horse-drawn coach. During the 1800s, however, all this changed. On 27 September 1825, crowds of people lined the 14-kilometre railway track that had been built between the towns of Stockton and Darlington to watch the first ever passenger steam train puff into view. Five years later, the world's first 'inter city' route was opened between Liverpool and Manchester, and by the turn of the century, Britain was covered with over 29,000 kilometres of railway track.

## 'SPUTTERING NOISY MONSTERS'

Many people dreaded the coming of the railway. Some thought that the 'hammering and roaring and hissing' of the steam trains would lead to milkless cows and eggless hens. Others thought that the engine sparks would set fire to crops. Yet, in spite of these objections, gangs of men called navvies were ordered to dig and blast their way across the countryside, leaving a criss-cross of tunnels, embankments and bridges behind them.

The arrival of the railways had a huge impact on the lives of everyone in Britain. Towns sprang up around the places where trains were built; industrial cities grew even bigger as soon as there was a railway to carry their factory-made goods; and ports too far away from the tracks simply dwindled and died.

▲ *The Victorians loved over-the-top decoration. St Pancras Station in London, opened in 1868, looks more like a great church than a railway station.*

Speedy train travel also meant that large amounts of fresh foods could be sent long distances without going rotten. And news, that had once taken days to get from town to country, could arrive in a matter of hours.

## ALL ABOARD
In the early days of railways, no one paid much attention to passenger comfort. First class carriages had seats, a roof and covered sides, but second and third class carriages were more like open cattle trucks. Unlike second class passengers, those travelling third class had nothing to sit on. Instead they had to hang on tightly to a handrail to stop themselves tumbling over the sides. No wonder railway company reports were full of references to passenger accidents!

▲ Railway companies offered cheap fares to the seaside. This meant that even the poor could afford to hop onto a train and enjoy an afternoon out by the sea.

### LET YOUR BRAIN TAKE THE STRAIN
The distance between London and York by train is 303 kilometres. In 1840 the journey took 11 hours. The train travelled at an average speed of approximately 27.5 kilometres per hour.

In 1893 the journey took 3¾ hours, at an average speed of about 81 kilometres per hour.

In 1993 the journey took 2 hours.

**a.** What was the average speed of the 1993 train?
**b.** In the 2 hours the journey took in 1993, roughly how far would passengers in 1840 have travelled? (Answers on page 30)

The introduction of steam-powered machines and the building of the railways created a great demand for iron, steel and coal. Iron and steel were needed to build machinery and railway tracks. Coal was needed to smelt the iron and steel and to provide fuel for steam engines.

# TRAMS AND TRANSPORT

## STEAM AND SAILS

The first successful steamships were built in the early 1800s, and by the late 1830s they were steaming their way across the Atlantic Ocean. Although the early steamers had sails, they didn't have to rely on winds. This made them quicker and more reliable than the sailing ships of old, and so helped to bring the most far-off lands within reach of Britain.

*Electric trams ran on rails in the street and were powered by overhead cables. Introduced in the 1890s, they soon put horse-drawn omnibuses out of a job.*

## HORSE POWER

Wealthy Victorians without their own carriages often hired horse-drawn taxis called hansom cabs or growlers. The first buses, called omnibuses, appeared in London in 1829. Pulled by horses, with seats both inside and on the roof, omnibuses were cheaper than cabs, but still too expensive for the poor.

8

## ON YER BIKE!

By the end of Victoria's reign, electric trams were adding to the chaos on city roads; electric underground trains were speeding about beneath London's streets; and low-framed safety bicycles were being ridden all over the country. During the late 1880s, cycling became all the rage as bicycles with equal-sized wheels and air-filled tyres were introduced. Two-seater bicycles, called tandems, were popular too, as this Victorian song suggests.

*Daisy, Daisy, give me your answer true.
I'm half crazy, all for the love of you!
It won't be a stylish marriage,
I can't afford a carriage,
But you'll look sweet
Upon the seat
Of a bicycle made for two!*

*This tandem bicycle dates from the 1880s.* ▼

*The modern motor car was invented in the late 1800s. The first cars in Britain were not allowed to go faster than 6.5 kilometres per hour and each car had to have someone walking ahead of it, to warn others of its approach.*

## BRIGHT IDEAS

Although the ancient Greeks knew about electrical forces, it wasn't until the Victorian age that electricity was used for lighting, communication and power. Electric street lighting first appeared in London in 1878, and by 1931 about half the homes in England had their own electricity supply. (Victorian homes without electricity were lit by oil or gas lamps and candles).

By the time Victoria died, electricity was also being used to send messages by telephone. Telephones were not a huge success at first because they were expensive, and many people were shy of using them. Wealthy Victorians left their servants to answer the telephone, to save themselves the embarrassment!

9

# THE BRITISH EMPIRE

When Victoria came to the throne in 1837, Britain already controlled a mighty empire which included parts of India and Canada and all of Australia. By 1901, this empire included the rest of India, most of Canada and parts of Africa and the Far East as well. These countries were known as the colonies. They provided the Victorians with tea, sugar and other foods which cannot be grown in Britain. They also supplied raw materials like wool and cotton which British factories made into goods. These goods were then sold to other parts of the empire for a huge profit. Without these trading links, Victorian Britain wouldn't have become nearly as wealthy or powerful as it did.

*The British Empire in 1901. Britain won control of most of her colonies by fighting for them.*

## THE BRITISH ABROAD

Hundreds of British people were sent to the colonies to govern them. Many more moved voluntarily to Australia, Canada and New Zealand because they wanted a better life for themselves, away from Britain's overcrowded cities. After the failure of Ireland's potato crop in the 1840s, nearly a million Irish people moved to America to escape starvation.

Like their countrymen back home, the Victorians who lived in the colonies were convinced that 'Britain Was Best'. As a result, they refused to fit in with the local way of life and often behaved as though they had never left Britain.

*This picture, which was painted in the early 1850s, shows a group of Victorians on their way to Australia. Can you spot where the couple at the front of the picture are sheltering their baby?*

10

# A MODEL QUEEN

When Victoria became Queen, the monarchy was in a bad way. The previous king, William IV, had made himself unpopular by meddling in political affairs. And the king before him, George IV, had been a rotten husband, a greedy eater and a drunk. According to one eyewitness, George IV ate so much that when he undid his corset his belly flopped down to his knees!

By contrast, Victoria was a saint! She neither interfered too much in politics, nor behaved badly. Instead she and her husband, Albert, worked hard, lived simply and spent much of their spare time with their nine children. After the scandalous goings-on of previous monarchs, Victoria and Albert's devotion to each other was a welcome change, and their example of family life was one which many Victorians tried to follow.

## SPILLS AND THRILLS

As a young woman, Victoria often spent her evenings playing spillikins with her Prime Minister, Lord Melbourne. To play your own version of spillikins . . .

**You will need:** a small matchbox full of **used** matches or a packet of cocktail sticks ● a piece of paper with a circle, measuring 10 cm across, drawn on it ●2 or more players

Spillikins or spellicans became popular in the mid-1800s when sets were often made from bone or ivory in the shape of tools and weapons.

▲Victoria and Albert made the royal family popular. Their mixture of ordinariness and wealth made it easy for prosperous Victorians to identify with them and respect them.

In 1861 Albert died of typhoid fever. In memory of her husband, Victoria had a bridge, a memorial and a round hall built in London, all of which are called . . . Albert. ▶

## THE RULES OF THE GAME

Each player takes a match and the rest are scattered inside the circle.

The first player then tries to pull a match out of the circle using his/her matchstick or fingers. If another match is moved by mistake, the first player stops and the next player has a go. If the first player removes a match from the circle without disturbing any of the other matches, he/she has another go.

The winner is the player with the most matches at the end of the game.

# LIFE UPSTAIRS

Victorian society was divided into three social groups or classes.

## UPPER CLASS

Upper class families were immensely rich and powerful. Many of them owned thousands of acres of land each, which they rented out for a profit, and had a house in town as well as one in the country. Most upper class parents didn't have to work. Their homes and land were looked after by servants, their food was prepared by cooks, and their children were cared for by nannies and taught by governesses. In fact, some young children spent so much time with their nannies and governesses that they knew them better than their own parents.

## MIDDLE CLASS

The middle class was made up of a wide range of people, from wealthy bankers, lawyers, factory owners and doctors to less wealthy shopkeepers, clerks and school teachers. All middle class men had to work to support their families, but unlike the working class below them, they never did physical work, such as laying railway lines or working in factories.

▲ Children from wealthy families spent a lot of time in their nurseries.

Many middle class Victorian families lived in houses still used today.▶

## KEEPING UP APPEARANCES

The middle class adored the royal family and longed to be considered 'respectable' like their Queen. They dressed smartly every day, kept their homes neat and tidy, and made sure that they did nothing that would shock their neighbours. Many of them also spent hours reading improving books which told them the correct way to do everything, including how to eat cheese!

'When eating cheese, small morsels (pieces) of cheese should be placed with a knife on small morsels of bread, and the two conveyed (carried) to the mouth with thumb and finger, the piece of bread being the morsel to hold as the cheese should not be taken up with the fingers, and should not be eaten off the point of the knife. As a matter of course, young ladies do not eat cheese at dinner parties.'
(*Manners and Rules of Good Society 1888*)

*Middle class families crammed their living rooms with as many ornaments and pieces of furniture as they possibly could. Servants responsible for dusting these rooms must have hated them with a vengeance!*

## FATHERS AND MOTHERS

Middle class family life was ruled by the father. He earned the money which was needed to feed his family and made most of the important decisions relating to them. Middle class wives were expected to obey their husbands, look after their children and organise the day-to-day running of their homes. Some wives also helped their husbands run the family business. Others just helped their maid with the household chores. Those wives with more than one servant often found themselves with nothing to do each day but call on friends, play the piano and make endless bits and pieces for the home.

*Many unmarried girls from poor families went to work as live-in servants. Their chores included lugging heavy scuttles of coal upstairs for fires, and washing their employers' clothes by hand.*

13

# PRESSING PETALS

When they weren't busy bossing their servants about or chatting with friends, wealthy wives often made pressed flower arrangements.

**You will need:** blotting paper
- freshly picked common flowers and leaves • a wooden board
- some large heavy books • glue
- a large sewing needle • thin card
- clear varnish • paint brush

Pressing works best if you use dry, fairly flat plants.

Always try to put plants of a similar thickness on the same piece of blotting paper. Large flowers will stop the books pressing down on smaller flowers and leaves.

**5.** If you want to use your pressed flowers to make a greeting card or bookmark, cut the card to the right shape, glue a flower design on the front and brush some varnish over it.

▲ **1.** Lay a sheet of blotting paper on top of the wooden board. Arrange the flowers and leaves on the paper, leaving a space between each one.

**2.** Lay a second sheet of blotting paper over the flowers and leaves.

**3.** Put the board in a place where it won't be moved and pile the books on top of it.

**4.** After about two weeks, lift up the books and the top sheet of blotting paper and carefully remove your dried plants. Use the needle to lift them off if they are stuck.

# CHILDREN AT WORK

For many of those who worked in Britain's factories, Queen Victoria's reign was a period of crippling poverty. To keep costs low, factory owners and other employers often paid unskilled workers very poor wages. This meant that whole families, including children, had to work long hours just to earn enough money to eat. One father told a government committee in 1830 that when the mills were busy his daughters worked from 3 a.m. to 10 p.m. By the time they got home the girls were so tired that they fell asleep with their supper still in their mouths.

*Very young children were useful in cloth-making factories because they were small enough to crawl under machines that were still running.*

## WOMEN AND CHILDREN FIRST

Looking after factory machinery was an unskilled job, so many bosses preferred to employ women and children because they could be paid lower wages than men. The conditions in which these women and children worked were often dreadful. The moving parts of the machinery were rarely covered, so horrific accidents were common. And the long hours spent in dark, dusty, noisy factories meant that many children grew up weak and sickly.

Factory children were not the only young workers to suffer great hardship. Before 1842 it was legal for children under ten to work underground in dark and dangerous coal mines. And up until the 1860s and 70s, many master chimney sweeps found it easy to ignore the law and send young boys up narrow, winding chimneys to brush out the soot.

*Very young children worked down coal mines, opening and shutting doors to let coal trucks through. In 1842 a seven-year-old, working down a pit in Sheffield, described his job thus: 'I stand and open and shut the door; I'm generally in the dark and sit me down against the door . . . I never see daylight now except on Sundays.'* ▼

*Poor parents who worked from home were helped by their children. This photograph taken towards the end of Victoria's reign shows a London mother and her children making brushes.*▼

*When my mother died I was very young
And my father sold me while yet my tongue
Could scarcely cry 'weep!' 'weep!' 'weep!'
So your chimneys I sweep, and in soot I sleep.*

William Blake – 'The Chimney Sweep'.

## CHOP AND CHANGE

During the course of Victoria's reign, laws were passed to improve poor working conditions. Some of these laws tried to stop young children from working (see pages 28 – 9). Others tried to make factory machinery safer and to ensure that workers received sick pay. These reforms did much to improve the workers' lot and, although working conditions in many industries were still bad in 1901, they were much better than they had been in 1837.

# CITY SLUMS

During the 1800s, many workers lived in rows of 'back-to-back' houses which were built close to the factories where they worked. Dreary, damp and overcrowded, these houses had neither piped water nor indoor toilets. Instead families had to collect their water from street taps or rivers, and share outdoor 'toilets' with their neighbours. These 'toilets' were often no more than a seat built over a pit in the ground. The smelly waste which collected in the pits was removed after dark by 'night soil men' and sold to farmers for fertiliser.

As there were no proper sewers, dirty water and human waste were often left to drain away in the streets. When this muck, along with factory waste, seeped into the water supplies, those that drank the water often caught dreadful diseases like cholera and typhoid.

*Smoke from factory chimneys, railways and household chimney pots made city slums dark and grimy. According to one Victorian reformer smoke made London 'the unsightliest metropolis in Europe'.* ▼

## CLEANING UP

As the Victorian age progressed, the government took steps to improve workers' living conditions. Underground pipes were built beneath the streets to carry away sewage, and town councils were made responsible for collecting refuse, re-developing slum areas and supplying clean drinking water. Since illness spread by city pollution sometimes threatened those living outside slum areas, the rich benefited from these changes too.

*Workers' houses were shockingly overcrowded. Sometimes an entire family had to live in just one room.*

# SCHOOLDAYS

In early Victorian times, many children did not go to school. A variety of schools were provided for them, but since schooling was not compulsory, and rarely free, many poor children did not attend.

## SCHOOL RULES

After 1870 the government set up schools in areas where there were none, and said that all children between the ages of five and ten had to go to school. In 1899 the school leaving age was raised to twelve. At first, most pupils attending the new schools had to take a few pence each week to pay for their education, but after 1891 all fees for these new schools were abolished.

## CHALK AND TALK

Victorian school work was far from fun. Pupils learnt the 3 R's every day – Reading, wRiting and aRithmetic – and spent a lot of time either copying words written on the blackboard or writing down passages read out by their teacher. Discipline was very strict and those who dared to misbehave were often beaten with a cane or a leather strap.

One Victorian schoolmaster was so strict, he used to punish his pupils by banging their heads together. His skull-shattering career came to a sudden end, though, when his right arm became paralysed.

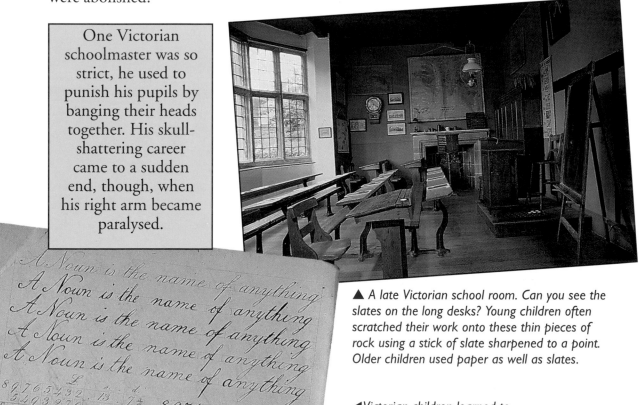

▲ A late Victorian school room. Can you see the slates on the long desks? Young children often scratched their work onto these thin pieces of rock using a stick of slate sharpened to a point. Older children used paper as well as slates.

◄ Victorian children learned to write by copying out sentences from copybooks. The size and shape of their letters had to be exactly the same as those printed in their copybooks.

18

# STITCH! STITCH! STITCH!

Upper and middle class sons were often sent away to privately run, fee-paying schools. Their sisters, however, were not considered important enough to be educated properly. Instead they were usually kept at home and taught skills that might help them to attract a husband.

One of these supposed 'husband catching' skills was sewing, and girls practised their stitches by embroidering letters of the alphabet, texts or numbers. These pieces of embroidery, which could take months to complete, were called samplers.

To make your own sampler

**You will need:** canvas (3 holes to each centimetre is a good size)
● embroidery silks or wool ● pencil
● tapestry needle ● scissors
● graph paper

**I.** Work out the spacing of your design on a piece of graph paper.

**2.** Copy your design onto the canvas using cross stitch.

**3.** To finish, oversew the outside edges of your sampler.

## CROSS STITCH

To make a cross, pull the needle out through hole 1, and push it down through hole 2. Then bring it out through hole 3, and push it down through hole 4.

To make a second cross, bring the needle out at hole 3 and repeat as before.

## OVERSEWING STITCH

Push the needle through from the back of the canvas and pull the thread through. Repeat until all the edges of your canvas are oversewn. Try to keep your stitches even.

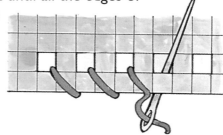

The sampler shown below was first oversewn in red, and then in green.

## DOUBLE CROSS STITCH

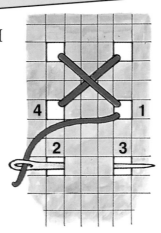

Sew a cross stitch across three holes instead of two. Then bring the needle out at hole 1 and put it in hole 2. Bring the needle out at hole 3, and put it in hole 4.

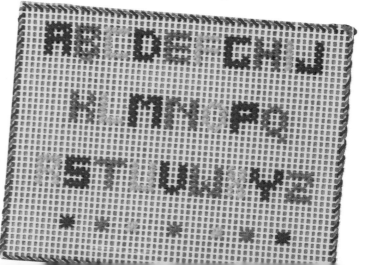

# DINNER IS SERVED

With cooks and servants to prepare their food, the upper class ate very well. Their meals were served on huge dining tables, decorated with flowers and ornaments, and their cutlery, glasses and china were the very best that money could buy. Upper class dinners were often made up of many courses. For guests of the Duke of Marlborough, a dinner consisting of soup, followed by fish, followed by an entrée, followed by a meat dish, followed by a sorbet, followed by game such as pheasant or duck, followed by a dessert, followed by a hot savoury, followed by a selection of fruit . . . was not unusual!

## FOOD FACTS

For the comfortably off, the Victorian age brought some welcome developments. Factories started producing kitchen equipment and coal-fired stoves which made cooking easier; by the turn of the century all major towns were linked by railway track, so fresh food could be sent quickly around the country by train; and from 1880 onwards, newly developed refrigerated steam ships brought in cheap meat, butter and fish from abroad. The arrival of cheap imported foods was good news for better-paid workers because it meant that they could afford a much more balanced diet.

*Families without stoves often took their meat to the baker's shop to be cooked.*

*A middle class Victorian kitchen. Coal-fired iron stoves called ranges had ovens built into the sides and a hot surface on top for kettles and pans.*

*An upper class kitchen in the early 1900s. The servants shown here were only a few of those that worked in this very wealthy home.* ▼

## DEADLY DIET

Although the diet of many working class people had improved by the end of Victoria's reign, it was never as varied as that of the upper or middle classes. For many poor city families, meals consisted mainly of bread, potatoes, cheese, tea and porridge with perhaps a bit of bacon when they could afford it.

Worse still, until foods were properly checked for safety standards, many Victorians were at the mercy of corrupt shopkeepers who watered down their milk and added plaster to their flour and sulphuric acid to their vinegar.

## MEASLY MEALS

Homeless families with nowhere to go except the parish workhouse probably had the worst diet of all. In return for work, such as breaking stones and crushing bones for glue, they were given a roof over their heads and cheap foods such as gruel. Gruel is a soup-like porridge made by boiling oatmeal in water or milk. Served with a slice of bread, it is one of the most revolting meals imaginable.

*During the Victorian age, manufacturers began to use brand names and easy-to-remember symbols, so that shoppers would recognise their products.* ▼

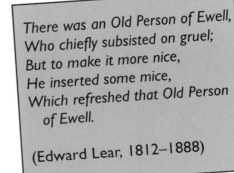
There was an Old Person of Ewell,
Who chiefly subsisted on gruel;
But to make it more nice,
He inserted some mice,
Which refreshed that Old Person
    of Ewell.

(Edward Lear, 1812–1888)

# JUST DESSERTS

Summer puddings were very popular in Victorian times. If you would like to make one for your family or friends . . .

**You will need:** 675 g of mixed summer fruits, such as blackberries, blackcurrants, redcurrants, raspberries and blueberries ● 4 – 5 tablespoons of granulated sugar (more if you have a sweet tooth) ● about 9 medium slices of white bread ● a wide, heavy saucepan ● a sieve ● a soup bowl or similar ● a litre pudding basin ● a knife ● 500 g weight ● a dinner plate ● a saucer or small plate that just fits inside the top of the basin ● an old shirt or plastic apron

If you don't have a 500 g weight, use a couple of tins, paint pots, etc, that weigh 500 g or more. Serves 6 – 8.

▲ 1. Put on the apron. Remove any fruit stalks and wash the fruit.

2. Place all the fruit except the raspberries in the saucepan with the sugar. Stand the pan over a low heat and cook gently for 10 minutes, until the sugar has dissolved and the juices run. Shake the pan occasionally, but don't stir the fruit or it will lose its shape.

3. Remove the pan from the heat. Add the raspberries and leave the fruit to cool.

▲ 4. Cut the crusts off the bread. Then cut a circle of bread to fit the bottom of the pudding basin and use some of the remaining bread to line the sides. Overlap the slices of bread and press the edges together, to make sure that there are no gaps between the slices.

5. Ask an adult to help you strain the fruit and collect the juice in the soup bowl.

▲ 6.Take the bread out of the pudding basin. Quickly dip it in the juice, to colour it, and then re-line the basin.

22

▲ **7.** Half-fill the lined basin with fruit. Cut a circle of bread to fit the middle of the basin. Dip it in juice and place it on top of the fruit.

▲ **8.** Add the rest of the fruit and put a layer of bread, dipped in juice, on top. Trim the bread if necessary to make a nice, neat finish.

▲ **9.** Lay the small plate/saucer on top of the basin and weight it down. Put the pudding in the fridge and leave it overnight.

▲ **10.** When you are ready to eat your summer pudding, turn it out carefully onto the dinner plate. Pour over any remaining juice, cut into wedges and serve with whipped cream or thick natural yoghurt.

  If you have trouble turning out your pudding, slide a thin bladed knife around the inside of the basin, to loosen the bread.

# RELIGION AND DOUBT

## SOLEMN SUNDAYS

Most middle class Victorians were practising Christians. They held daily prayers at home, said grace before each meal and went to church or chapel every Sunday – sometimes two or three times. Religious families kept Sunday as a day of rest and prayer. After church, children were often expected to sing hymns, go for a walk with their parents or play quietly. In very strict households, children were not even allowed to play silent games. In fact, some families considered Sunday so holy that they turned their paintings to the wall, and spent the whole day studying and praying.

Many upper and working class Victorians were also practising Christians. Very poor families living in slums, however, didn't have time to go to church. Even if they had, they probably wouldn't have gone because they had no decent clothes to wear.

*Victorian cartoons and newspapers often misunderstood Darwin's ideas and suggested that humans are descended from living apes, rather than long-extinct ones.*

## DARWIN'S BOMBSHELL

In 1859, a biologist called Charles Darwin stunned Christians everywhere by publishing a book which suggested that the Earth has developed slowly over millions of years, and that animal and plant species change over time. Until 1859, most Victorians believed that God had created the world in six days, as the Bible taught, and that the natural world was as it had always been. Since Darwin's scientific findings clearly went against biblical teaching, some Christians simply refused to believe his book. Others, however, were so disturbed by his ideas that they completely lost their faith in God.

THE LION OF THE SEASON.
ALARMED FLUNKEY. "MR. G-G-G-O-O-O-RILLA!"

24

# CRINOLINE CRAZY

By our standards Victorian clothes were formal and uncomfortable, particularly those worn by women and girls. To make their waists seem slim, Victorian females put on boned corsets which were sometimes pulled so tight, they felt like an instrument of torture. To make matters worse, in the 1840s and early 50s, women also wore lots of petticoats under their dresses, the weight of which must have made even the shortest stroll utterly exhausting.

During the 1850s, fashionable women of all classes abandoned some of their cloth petticoats in favour of a steel hooped underskirt called a crinoline. These cage creations, which hung from the waist like an upturned bowl, were covered with several layers of petticoat and a dress.

Crinolines varied in size from big to enormous. In fact, some of them were so huge that it was impossible for two crinolined ladies to walk into a room together without getting stuck in the

doorway. More embarrassing still, when pressure was put on one side of a crinoline's hoops, the other side shot upwards. No wonder 'respectable' women and girls wore long linen knickers under their dresses.

**Blooming Cheek!**
In 1851 an American called Mrs Bloomer came to England to try to persuade women to wear trousers. Her suggestion caused a storm of protest. It wasn't until the First World War (1914–1918) that wearing trousers became more acceptable for women.

# SPORT AND LEISURE

In early Victorian times, working people were expected to work every day except Sundays, Christmas Day and Good Friday. In 1863, many were given Saturday afternoons off as well.

In 1871 a law was passed which allowed banks to close on Boxing Day and for one day at Easter, Whitsun and in August. As very little business could be carried out whilse the banks were shut, these four 'bank holidays' soon became public holidays.

◀ *On public holidays, many families went on day trips to seaside towns such as Blackpool and Scarborough.*

*This is the Aston Villa team that won the F.A. cup in 1887.*▼

## FOOTBALL FANATICS

On their Saturday afternoons off, some workers went to the nearest public park to enjoy a bit of fresh air. Others set off to watch sporting events such as greyhound races or football matches. Until Saturday became a half day holiday, football was played mainly by public schools such as Harrow and Rugby. At first, the rules differed from school to school, especially on the question of whether players should be allowed to run holding the ball, but in 1863 the Football Association was founded and a definite set of rules were laid down. Those who agreed to these rules introduced the game to workers in industrial areas. Those who didn't played rugby instead.

The first famous football teams were founded by schools, churches, chapels and factories. Queen's Park Rangers began as a side from Droop Street School, while West Ham United was originally made up of men from the Thames Iron Works. (This is why West Ham are nick-named 'The Hammers'.) As the game became more popular, professional players were brought in, but unlike footballers today, they were paid no more than a skilled manual labourer.

*Derby Day by William Frith, painted in 1858. Rich and poor people alike loved to go to the races.*

## HOME-MADE FUN

Without televisions, radios or CD players to keep them amused, most Victorians had to make their own home entertainment. Middle class families often played games or read to one another in the evening. Wealthy households sometimes hired musicians to come play for them, while slightly less privileged families had to put up with their own piano playing instead! Working class people enjoyed music too, and many pubs put on musical entertainments.

For those wanting a cheap and cheerful form of public entertainment, the music halls took some beating. The shows put on in these halls featured all sorts of entertainers, from dancers, comedians and singers to acrobats, magicians and conjurors. By the end of Victoria's reign, music hall performers, such as Marie Lloyd, were as rich and famous as modern pop stars.

### Riddle dee dee
The Victorians loved trying to solve riddles like this one?
**Q:** *When is a bottle like Ireland?*

(Answer on page 30)

*In Victorian times, cricket was much more popular than football.* ▼

# TIME LINES

## INVENTIONS AND DISCOVERIES

### 1830s
1831 Michael Faraday makes discoveries which pave the way for electrical engineering. Two Englishmen invent the horse-drawn lawnmower.

### 1840s
1847 James Simpson discovers that a liquid called chloroform can be used to put patients to sleep safely during operations.

### 1850s
1851 Isaac Singer builds and markets the first sewing machine for use at home.

### 1860s
1862 By this date Louis Pasteur has discovered that disease is caused by germs. Before this discovery it was believed that many diseases were spread by smell.

## IMPORTANT EVENTS

1830 First inter-city rail route opens between Liverpool and Manchester.
1837 Queen Victoria comes to the throne.
1838 Morse code is used for the first time.

1840 Adhesive postage stamps used for the first time. Penny Post begins; Victoria marries her cousin, Albert.
1845 Fungus destroys Ireland's potato crop. About 1 million people die of starvation.

1854 British soldiers go to the Crimea to help the Turks fight against Russia. Florence Nightingale goes over to nurse the soldiers and on her return starts up the first training school for nurses.
1857 India tries to gain its independence from Britain, but without success.

1860 Horse-drawn trams are used for the first time.
1863 First underground railway opens in London.
1865 London becomes one of the first cities to build proper sewers.

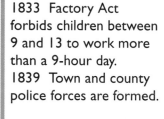

## REFORMS

1833 Factory Act forbids children between 9 and 13 to work more than a 9-hour day.
1839 Town and county police forces are formed.

1842 Women, girls and young boys no longer allowed to work underground.
1847 Women and children under 18 can only work 10 hours a day.

1852 Great Ormond Street Hospital for Children is founded in London.

1864 Young boys are no longer allowed to work as chimney sweeps.
1868 Groups of workers join together to form an organisation called the Trades Union Congress (TUC). United in this way, workers find it easier to improve their working conditions and pay.

## LEISURE AND PLEASURE

1838 Charles Dickens writes 'Oliver Twist'; Walter Wingfield invents a game called Sphairistike, which becomes lawn tennis.
1839 The first Grand National is run.

1841 Thomas Cook organises his first 'package' holiday from Leicester to . . . Loughborough.
1846 Edward Lear publishes his first nonsense poems.

1857 Thomas Hughes publishes his book 'Tom Brown's Schooldays'.
1859 Charles Darwin publishes his blockbuster 'On the Origin of Species'.

1863 Charles Kingsley writes 'The Water Babies', which tells the tale of a young chimney sweep who dies and comes back to life underwater.
1865 Lewis Carroll publishes his book 'Alice in Wonderland'.

## 1870s

1876 Alexander Graham Bell invents the telephone; Thomas Edison invents an early type of record player.
1878/9 Swan and Edison invent the electric light bulb.

## 1880s

1882 Robert Koch discovers the germ which causes tuberculosis. This was the first step towards discovering a cure for this deadly disease.
1886 Coca Cola is invented in America.

## 1890s

1893 Rudolph Diesel builds the first diesel engine. Diesel engines, which burn oil as fuel, are more efficient than steam-powered engines. Many modern vehicles have diesel engines.

## 1900s

1907 Bakelite, the first modern plastic is invented.
1908 Cellophane is invented.

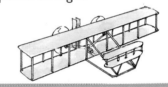

The first diesel engine

---

1870 Elizabeth Garrett Anderson becomes the first woman to qualify as a doctor in Britain.
1877 Queen Victoria is made Empress of India by her Prime Minister.
1878 William Booth founds the Salvation Army, which ran shelters for the needy.

1880 Cragside in Northumbria becomes the first house in the world to be lit by electricity.
1885 Karl Benz builds the first petrol-powered car.
1888 A mysterious murderer, nick-named Jack the Ripper, terrorises London.

1890 Opening of the Forth Bridge in Scotland, the world's first large steel structure; electric trams come onto the rails for the first time.
1895 X-rays are demonstrated for the first time.
1899 Boer War begins. Britons win this three year war against the Boers in South Africa, and Boer territory becomes part of the British Empire.

1900 The Labour Party is officially founded. Until the 1900s British politics was dominated by the Conservative and Liberal Parties.
1901 Queen Victoria dies and her son, Edward VII, comes to the throne.
1903 The Wright Brothers make the first powered flight.

---

1870 New Board schools are built in areas where there are not enough schools.
1874 Children under nine are not allowed to go to work.
1875 Town councils are made responsible for street cleaning and the supply of clean water.

1880 All children have to go to school until they are 10.
1882 Women are allowed to keep any wealth they are given as a gift or an inheritance. Before this a woman's husband was entitled to this wealth.

1891 Minimum working age is raised to 11; primary education in Board schools is made free.
1899 Children must stay on at school until they are 12.

---

1871 Bank Holidays are introduced.
1872 First ever FA Cup Final.
1873 Start of the cricket county championships.
1877 First Lawn Tennis Championship is played at Wimbledon.

1888 Football league is founded.

1896 First modern Olympic Games.

1902 Rudyard Kipling writes his 'Just So Stories'.

# GLOSSARY

**Arithmetic** – maths

**Back-to-back** – a house which backs onto another house so that neither of them has a back yard

**Biologist** – a scientist who studies living things

**Census** – an official count of population. A census has been taken in Britain every ten years since 1801, except for 1941, when Britain was at war with Germany

**Embankment** – a mound built to carry a level road or railway over a low-lying place

**Empire** – a wide-spread group of lands ruled by one powerful country

**Entrée** – a dish served at dinner between the main courses

**Industrial nation** – a country in which large amounts of goods are made in factories

**Industry** – a trade which produces large quantities of goods

**Manufacturer** – someone who makes goods on a large scale

**Memorial** – a statue, pillar, tomb, etc, built in memory of a person or an event

**Metropolis**– the capital of a country

**Mill** – a type of factory

**Monarch** – a king or queen

**Smelt** – to melt (one) in order to separate metal from other material

**Sorbet** – a frozen dessert made from fruit, water and sugar

**Transformation** – a change

**Answers:**
page 7 **a. 151.5 km/h** Average speed is worked out by dividing distance (303 km) by the time it takes to travel that distance (2 hours).

   **b. 55 km** We know the average speed of the 1840 train was approximately 27.5 km/h. Therefore, in 2 hours passengers would have travelled 2 x 27.5 = 55 km.

page 27 **A: *When it has a Cork in it!***

# Places to visit

Here is a list of just some of the many museums that have exhibits from the Victorian period. If you want information about the museums in your area, contact your local tourist board.

**Beamish**
The North of England Open Air Museum
Beamish
County Durham DH9 0RG
Tel: 0191 370 4000
*www.beamish.org.uk*

**Bradford Industrial Museum**
Moorside Road
Eccleshill
Bradford BD2 3HP
Tel: 01274 435 900

**Museum of Childhood**
Cambridge Heath Road
London E2 9PA
Tel: 020 8980 2415
*www.vam.ac.uk/vastatic/nmc/*

**Museum of Childhood, Edinburgh**
42 High Street
Royal Mile
Edinburgh EH1 1TG
Tel: 0131 529 4142

**National Coal Mining Museum**
Caphouse Colliery
New Road
Overton, Wakefield WF4 4RH
Tel: 01924 848 806
*www.ncm.org.uk*

**Cookworthy Museum**
The Old Grammar School
108 Fore Street, Kingsbridge
Devon TQ7 1AW
Tel: 01548 853 235
*www.devonmuseums.net*

**The Ironbridge Gorge Museums**
Coach Road, Coalbrookdale
Shropshire TF8 7DQ
Tel: 01952 884 391
*www.ironbridge.org.uk*

**Museum of London**
London Wall
London EC2Y 5HN
Tel: 0870 444 3852
*www.museumoflondon.org.uk*

**Nottingham Industrial Museum**
Courtyard Buildings
Wollaton Park, Nottingham NG8 2AE
Tel: 0115 915 3910

**National Railway Museum**
Leeman Road
York YO26 4XJ
Tel: 01904 621261
*www.nrm.org.uk*

**Ulster Folk and Transport Museum**
153 Bangor Road
Holywood, Co.Down
Northern Ireland BT18 0EU
Tel: 028 9042 8428

**Museum of Welsh Life**
St Fagans, Cardiff CF5 6XB
Tel: 029 2057 3500
*www.nmgw.ac.uk*

**York Castle Museum**
Eye of York
York YO1 9RY
Tel: 01904 687687
*www.yorkcastlemuseum.org.uk*

Every effort has been made by the Publishers to ensure that these websites contain no inappropriate or offensive material. However, because of the nature of the Internet, it is impossible to guarantee that the contents of these sites will not be altered. We strongly advise that Internet access is supervised by a responsible adult.

# INDEX

Additional Photographs:
Bradford Industrial
Museum P. 13; e.t. archive
P. 27; Hulton-Deutsch
Picture Library P. 8, 13, 21,
25; J. Allan Cash Ltd P. 6,
11, 21; The Mansell
Collection P. 4, 9; Mary
Evans Picture Library P. 7,
10, 11, 15, 24, 26; National
Trust P. 5, 12; Robert
Oppie Collection P. 21;
Salvation Army
International Heritage
Centre P. 16;
Warwickshire Museum P.
18.